"What is a more quintessentially American story than an alien space-craft crashing in the New Mexico desert in 1947? Rane Arroyo takes this story and writes a history not only of the event but of our country. There are cowboys, Indians, mayors, generals, J. Edgar Hoover—all in a painting of post-war paranoia and euphoria. Arroyo is half Norman Rockwell half Jackson Pollack, sketching photographically while splashing like a wild man. The reds of his small town nobodies merge with the blues of his own movieland dreams and the blacks and whites of what really happened. Or did it? Is Truth really Beauty? What can we know except this country is almost too weird to believe, but we open our eyes every day, and believe we must. *The Roswell Poems* is Americana at its most beautiful and bizarre."

BARBARA HAMBY, author of *Delirium* and *Babel*

"'The 20th Century is full of footnotes,' writes Rane Arroyo. In *The Roswell Poems,* the footnotes for Roswell, New Mexico, 1947, are written in couplets, in sonnets, in lyrical dramatic monologues, chatroom IMs, and imaginary film trailers. What happened in Roswell takes on 21st Century political significance in Arroyo's newest and most accomplished work, and reminds us that 'logic/ (is) a dreamer with holes in its pockets' and that 'mystery is/ one of the names that God wears.'"

KATHY FAGAN, author of *The Charm* and *MOVING & ST RAGE*

"Rane Arroyo's *The Roswell Poems* with sly brilliance create a 'memory foil' of poetry that pivots on a cowboy rancher discovering crash debris in the New Mexico desert. Arroyo dives down into that wreck and with his dream elegance of words, music, and psychological probing, exposes all the offbeat complexity of a land whose first peoples already knew about alien invasions. This book is a tour de force, interweaving individual stories with history, present time and future, with the mythic exerting its paradoxical truths and possibilities through it all. *The Roswell Poems* are America, right up to 9/11 and beyond. To read this book is to be abducted in heart-shaking and beautiful ways by Rane Arroyo's vision-craft."

SUSAN DEER CLOUD, recipient of the 2007 NEA Literature Fellowship and author of *The Last Ceremony*

THE ROSWELL POEMS

The Roswell Poems

Rane Arroyo

WordFarm

LA PORTE, INDIANA

OTHER BOOKS BY RANE ARROYO

Columbus's Orphan (1993)
The Singing Shark (1996)
Pale Ramón (1998)
Home Movies of Narcissus (2002)
The Portable Famine (2005)
How to Name a Hurricane: Stories (2005)
The Buried Sea: New & Selected Poems (2008)

WordFarm
2010 Michigan Avenue
La Porte, IN 46350
www.wordfarm.net
info@wordfarm.net

Cover Image: iStockPhoto
Cover Design: Andrew Craft
USA ISBN-13: 978-1-60226-001-6
USA ISBN-10: 1-60226-001-X
Printed in the United States of America
First Edition: 2008

Library of Congress Cataloging-in-Publication Data

Arroyo, Rane.
  The Roswell poems / Rane Arroyo.-- 1st ed.
    p. cm.
  Includes bibliographic references.
  ISBN-13: 978-1-60226-001-6 (pbk)
  ISBN-10: 1-60226-001-X (pbk)
  1. Unidentified flying objects--Poetry. 2. Unidentified flying objects--Sightings and encounters--New Mexico--Roswell--Poetry. [1. Roswell (N.M.)--Poetry.] I. Title.
  PS3551.R722R67 2008
  811'.54--dc22
                              2007051388

P 10 9 8 7 6 5 4 3 2 1
Y 14 13 12 11 10 09 08

ACKNOWLEDGMENTS

The Roswell Poems have been read and commented upon by readers, other poets and poetry audiences over many years. I was awarded an Ohio Arts Council Individual Excellence Award for 2007, an award that allowed me to complete this book.

While many historical figures are evoked in this work, I don't make any claims to represent these individuals faithfully; this is a work of fiction/ poetry.

I thank the many online guardians and skeptics of the Roswell Incident who've taught me much about passion. Benson Saler, Charles A. Ziegler, and Charles B. Moore's *UFO Crash at Roswell: The Genesis of a Modern Myth* informed this project in its 5th year.

None of these poems were published individually for I wanted them to be read together. Many thanks to WordFarm for supporting my vision as an artist, especially Marci Johnson.

To Glenn and the girls.

To the carriers of light in these dark days.

*To my students who know I praise and
envy them for their bright futures.*

*To Robert Heinlein, Ray Bradbury, Agatha Christie
and the other storytellers of my youth.*

CONTENTS

And what rough beast, its hour come round at last,
Slouches towards Bethlehem to be born?

William Butler Yeats, "The Second Coming"

INTRODUCTION

On July 1947, a cowboy rancher named Mac Brazel found crash debris from an airplane, weather balloon or a UFO in the desert. This chance discovery transformed the quiet town of Roswell, New Mexico into ground zero for theories of government conspiracies, space alien sightings, and science vs. religion debates. This sequence offers poetic constructions around a powerful mythic moment in contemporary culture and maps how an initial event moves far from its genesis. There was another nearby crash that was reported to have alien bodies. Soon in the mix were: possible illegal Nazis, government men, the Cold War warriors and Americans with spiritual crises. This work merges several timelines that offer various interpretation of "events," for contradictions define this "incident." The Roswell story/stories offer a new kind of mystery play in which everyone gets to participate— as believers, critics, or spectacle devotees. Something important happened in that obscure town, something happened that is still with us in the 21st century—but what?

BEFORE THE HOOPLA: 1946

Sleepy Roswell, New Mexico
isn't blooming with tourists yet.

Skies, and not waves, break
against a shifting landscape.

The town echoes of cowboy
boots and coyote alarm clocks:

English, Spanish and rattlesnake
hymns don't burden the miles.

A week's sweat work is rewarded
with illuminated beers in dull bars.

Roswell doesn't suspect that it's
to be the New World Bethlehem.

Its innocence will be pilfered, but
for now, trucks stir dust as they

race nowhere and arrive there.
Winds steal footprints and prayers.

UFOS OVER AMERICA

Radars read space and low clouds
    on blurry screens for it's the bold
age of science. Why then is logic
    a dreamer with holes in its pockets?
Above Roswell, White Sands and
    Alamogordo, objects pause before
hurrying off into the great black
    that surrounds this blued Earth.
UFOs complicate our alphabets
    as newspapers brag of raw crashes.
The Wright Brothers taught us that
    flight is our evolutionary future.

○ ○ ○

The young mock the unknown that
    hasn't known them yet. (Mystery is
one of the names that God wears.)
    Post-war skies are full of wonders
and winking signs as America,
    despite its homespun Christianity,
can't explain away all sky traffic.
    Weather balloons do look like
skulls when they linger in profound
    heights, but what is it that, though
wingless, won't yield to gravity?
    Invasion is not the boy-next-door.

○ ○ ○

There's a crash in Circleville, Ohio—

when did the Earth get mysterious?
There are photos of silver wreckage,
    an elephant after tusks have been
pulled out. Soon, grinning soldiers
    are featured in impure newspapers.
The young mock the unknown as if
    being jaded is a talent, a need.
The exposé is a choreographed
    spectator sport, a modern mirror in
which we see ourselves as mortals
    long abandoned by wide-eyed angels.

OUTSIDE OF THE CITY LIGHTS

A crash becomes The Crash.
Hard roars are still heard

as far sounds, singing wounds.
The suddenness of it, the dream

seeking a dreamer, the hasty
splitting of the atom and Adam,

Heaven stuttering like a storm,
New Mexico aging without warning.

EYEWITNESSES

MR. AND MRS. DAN WILMONT:
There was an oval shape in the night,
a lump of coal on fire but not burning.

WILLIAM WOODY:
My father and I watched
a light with a red tail—a comet?
Satan's trail in one's stare?
It went Northwest, killed the compass.

MOTHER SUPERIOR MARY BERNADETTE:
We were changing shifts at
St. Mary's Hospital when
from the third floor windows
facing mountains, a fire grabbed
the horizon and nearly broke
its neck. I know that miracles
need holy approval from the See,
but I was the one who was there
doing the seeing—but I must have
blinked for all became black.

SISTER CAPISTRANO:
It was an undressed object in flames,
a threat to common sense: it was
a far roundness like a button falling
from the Virgin's dress, only
not that and more like a torch
seeking the shape of a human hand.

OTHER EYEWITNESSES:
The others stay quiet, cached in
their real fear of being mocked.
Some confess to priests that they
saw Satan smoking in the dark.
Some build bunkers against beasts
no longer abstract or far away.

ANONYMOUS (NURSING HOME STORY, 1995):
We were in his truckbed, naked,
lovers refusing to be zero. It was 1947,
the year of the matador. We were there,
laughing in the desert. Then glass
stars exploded, then a slow-motion
apocalypse that made us stop kissing.
It was a time when secrets thrived:
like us, the U.S., and the universe.
We leaned against each other and
glorified being human. Invasions,
evasions, visions. We made Heaven
crash! Yes, we were that beautiful.

MAC BRAZEL:
I heard a bookish bomb dropped from
an angel's slippery hands: BOOM!
A tune culled from the Alpha's tremors.

MAC BRAZEL TALKS TO THE POET, MAN-TO-MAN

A ranch manager like me shouldn't
become an American Ulysses, Buddha
in shit-kicking boots, or John Wayne's
stunt double. Sometimes I wake up
from yelling at the younger me as I close
my eyes to imagine the poised world.
A protagonist should be ageless and not
wear the weather of lost days on his
or her face. Anything can happen here
with or without God's permission.
Poet, don't turn me into Sisyphus and
make me saddle the sun again and again.

ENTER THE COWBOY

Mac Brazel and a 7-year-old child
find a debris field full of shine.

He's Jonah choosing a pickup truck
and not a ship as his escape from visions.

This crash has done the impossible:
it has sent ripples through a desert.

Mac returns home without absolutes.
The Proctors ask, is this sky flotsam?

One "little sliver" of silver can't be cut
or burned; he calls it memory foil.

The unknown exists without our
permission—how is that possible?

Chaves County is suddenly full of aliens
that don't speak Spanish, don't linger.

Mac's solar plexus has an eclipse.
Our cowboy tries to sleep but hears his

horses beg to be ridden where darkness
turns silver hooves into hard sparks.

PATRIOTIC CHAOS

This Fourth of July is ordinary
with sparklers, beer and erect flags.

The roar and the ours of the spectacle,
stars reading our writing for a change.

And the two-fisted provincialism
is showing-off to picnickers, off-duty

soldiers, and illegal workers who
wear the dripping fireworks like jewelry.

Mac waits days to tell of his sky fire.
Small towns love to burn spy effigies,

unholy lanterns of their own in darker
times. America outshouts its prophets.

THE FUSE IS LIT

This is Sheriff Wilcox and we found
something of yours that's lost and
it's on Brazel's land so maybe it's his
or maybe it's God's or maybe it's
a Martian toy and this is the Sheriff
with Brazel which isn't pronounced
like Brazil and he isn't the Sheriff
but a good man and his ranch is being
raided by something and this is Wilcox
so get here and illegals I can handle but
not from space so get here or I'll call
bored priests and the exorcising press
if you military boys can't act like men
because Brazel can't drive Satan out of
town by himself and I'm the Sheriff
but this isn't the wild west still and
yeah we're two-fisted but get here
and bring the prayers you can spare

MAJOR JESSE MARCEL RACES TO THE DEBRIS SITE TO TAKE NOTES

I speed towards the speculations

        alone. This daylight is relentless,

a harsh hammer full of harm.

        What a cruel sun. Road mirages

melt before my faithful gazes.

        To read a ruin requires a cold eye.

I know my script: *this isn't debris*

        from space, but more Soviet Union

puppetry. For now, I sing aloud,

        loose again and loving this day's

spilled fuel. Watch me burn down

        this goddamn planet with just

one wrong turn, one rash rollover.

        Ahead, work. Behind, work.

For now, I sing to the raw radio,

        young again, in love with distances.

THE WORLD OUTSIDE OF
ROSWELL EXISTS

The Marshall Plan is approved and ruins
are healed or hauled away. Europe learns
how not to be the world's chessboard.
Rosie the Riveter wears nylons again.

India and Pakistan declare themselves
fraternal twins as The Empire gets its ass
kicked by sun-blessed beautiful mobs.
The Hollywood "Black List" puts on boots.

Films are circumcised and resized to fit
the puppetry that is now citizenship.
A stamp costs 3¢. Tourists write home of
Broadway's New Orleans, un-shirted

Marlon Brando in *A Streetcar Named Desire*
and honor the testosterone that our nation's
foes would steal. Sartre's *Existentialism*
confirms that books are always bombs.

The Dead Sea Scrolls are given mouth
to mouth and maybe Jesus was a cultist
who needed an apocalypse of his own.
J. Edgar Hoover's shadow looms over D.C.

THE CANTING

Headlines: shipwreck in the sky,
Satan arrives on a flying disk,
military gives Martians a 21-gun-salute.

Daily Record says: no words on
the found metal tape, just flowers,
flowers from deep space, flowers

that must mean something or else
symbols are merely crypts.
(Can any good come out of Roswell?)

Mac wishes he could sing a hymn
or sing along to "Sugar Moon"
by Bob Wills and His Texas Playboys.

The cowboy says little after
he describes the dream debris.
When will he run out of words?

RELEASE

The first press release is unleashed:
flying disc dives headfirst into history.

Homesick soldiers run around needing
more war. Human energy rarely just

dissipates. AP wires sing like boys lost
in a cemetery as KGFL splits noon's

bones: *They're here! Where are they?*
What are they? Pray for us. The secret

anthill has been kicked by a military boot
and frenzy is rich fertilizer for black

budgets. It's true or it wouldn't be in
the papers: space beings pare bared skies.

Cover-ups court in tight pants as what is
released spreads wings and ushers storms.

RUMORS OF SPACE ALIENS (A SECOND CRASH AND COUNTING)

Roswell is a small town
        shrinking into
ground zero gossip.
        Illegal aliens are
left alone for days,
        replaced by Martians
and their kind,
        kindling for future
witch burnings.

Some have seen giants, walking fetuses, Satan's angels.
Some say the Nazis are birthing a super race in our desert.
Some say that God has sent us a plague for Darwin's folly.

        Everyone knows
someone who saw with
        his own eyes: stacks
of dead bodies,
        children of a broken
sky, a rhetorical
        aha, plague carriers
without souls.

○ ○ ○

The second crash plays second fiddle:
no photogenic cowboy, no ha ha and
oops. Some aliens were shipped in
children's caskets; the living ones,

are they in some secret scientific
circus? Are they being bred like
wild horses pulled back from the Void?
Do the un-winged dream of their home

planet of the green skies over green
mountains herding green rivers?
We prefer Brazel as flawed hero,
a sphinx made in our flawed image.

THE UNIFORM

Marcel stopped at his home to show
his wife pieces of his lack of peace.
Guards blocked all the roads near
the crash site. Tin soldiers now had

a calling, a purpose, a boredom they
had to keep to themselves or else be
thought of as unpatriotic, a wild leak.
Marcel breathed best in pure rooms

where his wife breathed. She gazed
at the metal, a complex spiritual bomb.
Marcel wanted to take off his uniform,
Adam and Eve it, watch for comets in

his wife's eyes. But the unbuttoning
didn't happen after Marcel thought of
soldiers guarding a mystery. He returned
to them, uniform as wrinkled as the day.

RUBBERNECKING AT THE CRASH SITE

All gawkers are turned away.
But a wounded land has wounded
people: Russians or space aliens?

Not disturbed Indian gods? Not
Mexicans hotwiring a patrol plane?
The MPs are like lost scarecrows

mourning farms buried by dull
dust storms. These are the first
tourists, but they can only mail

metaphysical postcards. Rumor is
starving. Military Orders are: *shoot
to kill what moves.* Even the moon?

NO MIDDLE GROUND

Generic General Twining makes
a surprise stop in Albuquerque.
For turquoise? For take-out tacos?
For a romp? Kirtland Air Field stands
at attention. The Eye of The East
is upon them all. It never blinks.
It's an unannounced visit—secret
annunciation, minus the religion.
It's now the era of Them versus Us.
The Russians and the Americans.
The Military and the Civilians.
It's team sports gone amuck.
Conspiracy has its first blooms.
The sky gets stolen in broad daylight.

BACK TO THE SCENE OF THE
COSMIC CRIME

The cowboy is in an airplane,
                suddenly an aerial bloodhound.
Mac is godeyed without training.
                Look for shininess. Look for
a pillaged landscape, disturbed sand.
                Brazel sees a Joseph and Mary
and son crossing the desert
                (¿José, María and singing niño?).
He won't give them up to the enemy,
                ah, to his own army. A simple
gesture: *Look, over there, it's unkempt*
                and the plane banks to the right.
His mirage is safe, for now, and Mac
                learns innocence is not a legal right,
that the debris field will never be
                decoded, that his story is no longer his.

HOUSE ARREST OR
GOVERNMENT GUEST

Mac is bad luck's poster boy.
He dreams of flying backwards

into space to offer falling stars
refuge in his softening skull.

There is no Pegasus to saddle.
The Crewcuts ask him to prove

that he's patriotic and say that he saw
no bodies, no wreckage, no sky shards.

Amnesia rarely offers amnesty.
You can't make me invisible, he says.

The interrogators frown,
since when do cowboys write poetry?

THE RECANTING

The *Roswell Daily Record* sells the tale:
weather balloon hijinks, hallucinations,
Russian hysteria, Messiah complexes.
It's in print. Mac wears soldiers and
guardian angels as if his best cologne.
Nothing is to be pure again as the cowboy's
ass is branded in daylight. Martyrdom is
photogenic in hindsight, always scripted.
Mac recants: *It was a weather barroom.*
Officers take back the first press release.
Jeeps full of metal—and alien bodies.
Officers press their presence at offices
to keep order—stir dust as they vanish.
Officers demand that there be no past.
There was weather. A balloon too. Me.
Officers are drunk with a secret's adrenalin.
It's the cowboy's turn to be saddled.
Officers impress with their uniforms of sweat.
No flying saucer, but a whether balloon.

TERRIBLE ANGELS

Sergeant Melvin Brown lifts a tarp:
bodies! But not the kind seen in
human wars. He has heard many

rumors. It's a thin line between
the kinetic and the truly frenetic.
Soldiers run about, guns aimed at

fierce stars, at florid shadows in
the floating dark. Something is
loose, less, but what? This is not

a traditional war—is it a war at all?
Brown drops the tarp and prays
that he hasn't been seen seeing.

Something is dead inside of him
as the denied bodies become cargo
for Ohio's Wright-Patterson Airbase,

or so he learns later from drunk pilots.
Who's plucked these terrible angels?
The 20th century is full of footnotes.

THE ACCIDENTAL MESSIAH

Mac has nightmares but they're
his, something to own and not to be

fingerprinted, sniffed, frowned at.
He's in a field and watches it wear

fire after a crash. But it's not what
happened. The cowboy showed up

in the aftermath of the abstract
wearing flesh. He's in a field and runs

to a silver ship turning into slivers.
He's in a field he sets on fire with

meaning. Mac can't stop the Earth
from turning into an unholy desert.

He chases his shadows on burning
horses as the sky tries to swallow him.

WHAT BEAST IS NOW AWAKE?

Planes come and go. Debris on some,
personnel on others. The beehive has

too much honey, the Pentagon's wet
dreams. More than one enemy!

Testosterone zone: no civilians
allowed. Planes weave but not blankets.

No trails. The smoke up Satan's ass
falls sown again. Toothy pilots. Not Pontius.

The air is heavy with sound, like music,
but with cargo too heavy to bear.

Winged mules. Brainwashed bees.
There is skywriting in invisible ink.

BAR TALK AMONG OFFICERS

Loss of faith isn't for civilians—
not yet, nyet. The skilled military
explains myths as if cosmic

errors within local judgments.
How will we deal with aliens
when we don't know ourselves,

no matter how many times we've
been naked? Grainy photos of
soldiers grinning and crouched

next to weather balloons in tatters
can remind us that we've survived
being young, that tomorrow's ruins

are where we live now. Let's drink
until our skulls glow, until they're
the sun's rivals. All eras are dark.

CONSPIRACY CHESS GAMES

Professor Lincoln La Paz is now
convinced the shards of the ship

aren't ours. A year earlier, FBI Hoover
ordered Linc to stop sniffing around,

that he swallow his rasping conclusions.
A ventriloquist's dummy must not

believe in free will and press conferences.
La Paz is one voice in a cover-up choir.

Entropy is the best assassin. Amnesia
spreads like a plague, but it's too late:

once information leaks, a flood is
born in slow motion, drop by drop.

The rumor is that we're Pavlov's
Pinocchios, brainwashed zombies.

Dr. La Paz fades away, but his ideas
root where they can, while they can.

Roswell suffers a sky change and
becomes a question and not a place.

MYSTERY PLAY REHEARSALS

Mac Brazel's two years of scrapping
metal is legally taken away when
he brags in uncrowned Corona that
he still has proof. He is poor now.
His last holy relics are confiscated,
Congressionally stored inside
classified information's asshole.
Slow whispers have been the start
of most world religions. Mac has
lost New Mexico's newness, old
Mexico's oldness. He's cursed or
blessed—the same thing? The poet
as pilgrim despairs: *What's left to
steal from a naked cowboy?* Plenty.

ROSWELL RETURNS TO SLEEP

No need for a magic spell for warfronts
always shift, change, chase other shamans.
Our cowboy watches the rigid desert

heal itself with chance winds and days
of slow light. Other sightings, other
theological debates with guns—elsewhere.

Roswell gives up adrenalin cold turkey.
Lacking Hollywood's chameleon skills,
the town learns the stern art of patience.

THE HOPI PURIFICATION DANCE: 1969

The Hopi have predicted that ships
without wings will unfurl themselves

after we steal moon rocks and other
lunar bric-a-brac. What can a poet do?

I'm fourteen and not strong enough
to throw those rocks back to the Luna.

While the Hopi dance, files are filled
with secrets. Puppetry is now normal.

Men in bunkers deny they've seen skies.
The Hopi send their shadows into space.

JESSE MARCEL, JR. FINALLY SPEAKS
OF 1947 (IN 1982)

My father stirred us up and I tried
hearing him and I thought I was awake
when he showed us the alien scraps
including the hieroglyphics, the symbols
representing something, almost half
Aztec and half mathematics and I asked—
am I dreaming or is this happening?—
and shivers ran through me, aliens from
cold space, and I've been awake now
for decades, survived the Cold War
and being awake isn't the same as being
aware, but I was aware of my father's
rough cheek as he rubbed my face and
whispered, my son, my heir, look, look,
see the universe and so I stared, seized.

TABLOID SPACE ALIENS

They're small, contemporary
leprechauns, Tolkien's hobbits

on the wrong Earth, children
with adult death ray toys.

They come to warn us about
space wars, the atomic bombs

we're hatching, our masters
from deep space's bad temper.

Some make babies to conquer
our species. Others frolic in

Las Vegas with show-off girls
(some in drag, but it's the 1980's

and there are more sties than eyes).
Some kidnap humans because

they left their lab rats back home
(where is home?). Somehow

they elude radar, the national
defense—but not tabloid

photographers who have
replaced St. John of Patmos.

THREE OTHER THEORIES

1. THE CIA
The military, space aliens and
the illegals struggle for good press:
Roswell is full of shiny-shoed ghosts,
men in white shirts taught not
to weep except through the armpits.
They are trained to grab shadows
by the short hairs until they sing.
Buzzcut chameleons breed shamelessly.
The CIA has been waiting for
the chance to play with marked
Tarot cards. Government agencies
believe that when two or more
are gathered there are seeds of
revolution ripe for the planting.
As WWII runs out of corpses and
conflicts, new fuel is necessary
to distribute mass hysteria. Space
aliens help our nation to keep
its eyes up toward questions. Yes,
we live in a paradise for pickpockets.

2. NAZIS IN THE AMERICAN DESERT
Operation Paperclip: let's bring
126 skimbled Nazi scientists
to the Southwest for aerial farming,
to pin tails on our rocket burros.
Soon, Roswell blossoms into a myth,
a señorita with swastika-print nylons.
Accident, synchronicity, or bad

community theater? Nuremberg was
for the fool without a bargaining chip
or a cyanide eyetooth. The Nazis
hate all this warmth, the lack of snow,
the cacti forests, the stink of pure air
not wearing Alpine cologne. They like:
tequila, being nude at pools just to scare
the figleafed Americans, budgeted
freedoms, and how blonde that daylight is
in this primitiveness so physical, present.
Imagine Wernher von Braun eating a taco!
(Padre of the V-2 rocket that felt up
England.) He's surrounded by brown
natives, savages, indigents, the future.
Mariachi bands learn to play *Lili Marlene*.

3. THE ATOMIC BOMB

Ah, Roswell, how often I would have
gathered you. Tired Isaiah asks in 33:14:
"Who among us shall dwell with everlasting
burnings?" Roswell houses atom bombs,
those eggs anxious to hatch, those shortcuts
to checkmate. It's on a need-to-know-basis
nest, secret cache of catastrophe. We've
wars and rumors of whores. Perhaps
God has sent us means for a cleansing.
The crash was a miscalculation. Complete
with mannequins as our stunt doubles.
Omega walks backwards towards Alpha.
Atom bombs snore until they become
historical fact, a storm beyond cause and
effect. Heights were once beyond human
sculpting. Now space is crowded with
the absences of gods and severe ghosts.

THE APOCALYPSE MENTALITY

Now we have ufologists, skeptics
that make Doubting Thomas

look like an extra in a musical,
post-Watergate junkyard dogs.

There are websites of Jesus
waving from Venus, stigmata

storm troopers, delivery service
to secret bunkers, coup-de-tat

couture camouflage uniforms,
intelligent design blaming Satan

for dinosaurs, cults riding to
the stars by suicide, and Roswell

returned to us in spit-and-polished
seven-league boots. Mapmakers

used to indicate where monsters
lived, which islands, which ruse

and now threats thrive in the air,
tap our phones, rewrite history

before it happens. Black budgets
underwrite top secret bestiaries.

CONSPIRACY FEVERS AFTER ROSWELL

Unmarked helicopters, cowled cows
slaughtered by men in wolf masks,
the whispers and the winks between
men in black who smoke in the black,
the ushering of why not, prime time
autopsies faked in generic railroad
cars, alien bodies stacked like firewood
(in the desert?), military greed for
front row seats at splashy Armageddon,
eyewitnesses from blind trailer parks,
suicides treated as personal dramas,
money trails to corporate Jacuzzis,
the vague van that stops at one's door—
it's the romantic CIA come-a-courting.

PADRE ALFONSO'S SERMON
ON SPACE ALIENS

Remember that Satán fell from the sky,
and from such great heights that when
he hit the Earth, he burrowed all the way

to Hell. That's the crash of all crashes!
What's happened here is nothing. Beware
of saviors with Mother Ships for the Virgin

needs only the technology of her Grace.
Our Lady of Guadalupe doesn't do aerial stunts.
Jesus was an Earthling, a handsome one who

didn't look like a sea turtle from space, who
didn't bring Salvation through the Pentagon's
back doors, who chose our planet to murder Him.

VISIBLE SOUVENIRS

for Marguerite Helmers

Yes, there is the business of selling
the rewritten past. We need endless

amounts of alien-with-lit-eyes pens.
All pilgrimages are defined by

pensiveness and one's expenses.
Once, Jesus' foreskin was sold in Europe,

many times and in many places.
Our script is about Doubting Thomas'

hard change of heart as we cling
to our incredulity until conversion.

Now, alien festivals in Roswell,
Mardi Gras for the mystery addicts,

a Day of the Dead for star visitors.
Tours, lures, impure science, sureties

that we're not alone in the implied cosmos,
unashamed of shaming governmental acts.

In the past. In the present now the past.
Others wait to be abducted, singled out.

Others just buy the T-Shirt that brags,
This cowboy can beat up your astronaut.

CHAT ROOM SEEDINGS

DIEGOLAMANCHA: Trust me, go to Roswell. P.S. Bring condoms & William Blake poems.

FAIRYBOAT: Diego's right. Also an empty suitcase. I sell T-Shirts on eBay. Saving up for past life therapy. I want to bottle Roswell air, anyone interested?

LULALUNA: Better than Disneyworld. I bought my children angel wings they still wear! :)

HOUSTONHOTTIEHANK: Spiritual place. But I'm half Hopi. Anyone else feel special there?

ZORROZERO: ¿Hola? Anyone else hated Roswell? Everyone was old there.

BETTYANDTHEJETS: I hear none of the hotels there have Bibles.

FAIRYBOAT: Luna, why not wings for u 2!

DIEGOLAMANCHA: Hey 3H, me 2. That's a big yes. Zorro, I'm in my 30's and not old.

99QUESTIONS: Is William Blake a folksinger? Roswell on TV wasn't blockbuster. Too cheesy.

FAIRYBOAT: Mac Brazel should be played by some Australian actor. They know the outdoors in that crazy country.

HOUSTONHOTTIEHANK: Anyone a shaman? Can't you hear me

through the machine?

BETTYANDTHEJETS: Diego you sound sexy. I got a single brother, hmmm.

ZORROZERO: I am legal age, hint.

LULALUNA: I'm from Wisconsin and I know cheese and Roswell was more caviar for the soul.

JUMPINGFIREMAN: I'm single, Big D. And Hottie, what we do at church is our own business.

FAIRYBOAT: What about the air? Bottles? Anyone had a miracle at Roswell?

99QUESTIONS: Tyger, tyger, burning bright

DIEGOLAMANCHA: IM me, got photos. All kinds. Can prove that I'm an Earthling. Even if not Australian.

JOJOTHEJUGGLINGWARRIOR: Just entered here. Anyone think Roswell was supposed to distract us from Disney making alien colonies in plain sight!

BETTYANDTHEJETS: Diego, every inch an Earthling?

JUMPINGFIREMAN: Mac was like Frodo. He lives!

FAIRYBOAT: I live alone, but I know we're not alone.

THE POET IS ALSO ENSNARED
BY THE MYTH

I dream that *The X Files*' Fox and I
are in a red Roswell motel when a force
lifts us into disturbed air. Too much
TV? Too little myth? He holds my
hand: *Come—the New World Bethlehem
waits for us.* But what was born here?
We run into an L.A. mad maze inside
amazement. Percussion hunts us down.
But Fox and I find a tunnel into Mexico
where a tall cathedral full of small coffins
glows, calls us—but not by our names.
A priest says, *sí, we saved some of the angels.
What is a shepherd without lost sheep?*
Fox whispers, we conquered this planet,
we're the unforgiven trespassers, we kiss.
Why does evil and not we know that poems
have powers? I lean against Fox: we're real.

AFTER ANOTHER ALIEN FESTIVAL

Finally, the hotels quiet down
as pilgrims slip into dreams of

alien angels. Lonely sheriffs
cruise around as grunts for

hide-and-seek gods. Are threats
coming tonight from the skies,

the desert, or the drunks in
Martian masks? I watch

low-riders in neon cars circle
and circle like penitents around

a saint's rumored ashes in a box
in a dim cathedral. There are

too many mysteries to solve in
one lifetime, one night, one poem.

GRANT NARRATIVE TO SUPPORT
THE ROSWELL POEMS

In childhood, I had Godzilla.
In puberty, I had The Astronauts.

In my twenties, I had Joseph Smith.
In my midlife, I have Roswell

(am I in the middle of my life?).
I love the cowboy, the aliens

(of this world and other worlds),
the mess of it, the struggle for

clarity in darkening times, again—
the lit city on the hill. When we

(if we) go to Mars, we will be
the space aliens, Señor President.

The Roswell Poems are for those
neglected by poets: the masses.

We're still apes in love with gods:
The Burning Man, drug concerts,

Graceland, and, of course, Roswell.
The sky falls. We resurrect it.

Science fiction is now a modern
chapel, laboratory, or a grotto.

In my grave, kept from starlight,
I'll have the Conqueror Worm.

ROSWELL: THE TELEVISION SERIES

Left behind as beautiful teenagers,
they lose virginity after virginity
while learning to speak and pout.

They share with homo sapiens,
a confusing puberty, friction's
facts, and angst worthy fan clubs.

Their Roswell is complicated by
rivals at high school and by dark
government witch killers. The actors'

perfect eyebrows are rhetorical
questions, their bodies each other's
plots. Yes, who hasn't been an alien

in a back seat, skies yielding to
the falling kisses? These rebels
praise gravity's role in making love.

HALLOWEEN IN TIME OF WAR

The first trick-or-treaters are
a skeleton, a pregnant princess,

a naive raccoon. Thank you,
they say while racing back to

their trance dance down glowing
streets. None are dressed as our

sordid president. None use an Iraqi
skull as their goofy goody bag.

Hola, Harry Potter knock-off,
ballerina with a parent in pink,

GI Joe with a flag bandana.
The dead have been upstaged again.

Mourning them is left for us who
have little altars for our vast griefs.

How strange to be drunk on oxygen.
I think of children in Roswell

wearing human masks, how they
must tire of aliens hiding in mirrors.

DREAM

Oh, history involved itself
Sufjan Stevens, "Concerning the UFO
Sighting Near Highland, Illinois"

Roswell's illegal aliens look up at
a UFO or is it the Madonna returning
without green cards for them?

A posse is forming, cowboy hats in
blonde hands, and one of our country's
tragedies is that we are clichés with

crotches that aren't psychic. As if
fist fighting with the stars makes sense,
as if the 1940's are a permanent scar.

You, reader, and I, grab hands and
run towards a nearby crash that's cash
in the bank for government conspiracy

prophets: it's a volcano's diary, Roswell
becoming Roswell. How to explain
the profound loneliness of that desert

and the rose of truth as Yeats demanded
of his muse? Contrast is a love letter
never mailed, never composed because

of a surprise storm, never for human
language. But how we try to write it
before it writes us as merely chance
eyewitnesses to the history of our lives.

Reader, thank you, for throwing your
arms around me and bringing me back

to this glowing verb from outer space.
Auden, did you ever see America this
naked? D.H. Lawrence, did you in

your "ghost" ranch? This is only a dream,
or not. The hombres in black chase us
for refusing to be blind citizens and

I never imagined writing about Roswell
would be so sweaty. Bodies are being
carried to albino trucks and we're

suddenly fluent in Spanish, mistaken
for illegal workers propping this palace
of cards. Reader, I save your life so

you will read. I return to Roswell where
myth and muscle battle for narrative's
throne, where meaning waits a lover.

LETTING GO

This is an open adiós to the cowboy
for I'm thinking of you again, Mac Brazel—

a visit? an obsession? an accusation?
But if I let you fade, then…then…
I already ache for our sun's death, but then,
Mac, we're a species that builds museums

to evoke ourselves; much survives doubts.
We're in a mystery play, surprised to be

the mysteries. All the cowboys of my life
have prepared me for your quiet presence.

Mac, Roswell was ground zero for faith
and doubt to battle, and you were a prophet

by the bad luck of being. Much has changed
since the 1950's furtive sex lives seemed

the only way out of public hurrahs. Earth
is smaller, a tender music note, a shy bud

in the paradise of multi-dimensional uni-
verses. I know amigo, how is the future

to be ever saddled? What shines, sometimes,
hurts when we become blind and prosaic.

I'll bring gossip about the cosmos, soon,

when I sink into Earth, when I lose the sky's

shining promises. A crash may happen
quickly but its wreckage is ours forever.

A MOVIE TRAILER FOR
THE ROSWELL POEMS

VISUAL:
A cactus flower is suddenly
bathed in green light.

VOICE OVER:
Remember: no day is
ordinary or a dream.

VISUAL:
A silver airship crashes
into the sleeping desert.

Voice Over:
Pious heights are
full of vigilant spies.

VISUAL:
People pour out of their houses:
telescopes, rosaries, puppets.

VOICE OVER:
Roswell, New Mexico, is
startled by its celebrity.

VISUAL:
The town reverberates as
the military runs about with
raw guns and shouting to
shadows with walkie-talkies.

VOICE OVER:
Some storms wear weather
that weather the soul

VISUAL:
Mac is on his mad horse
looking at a shining wreck.

VOICE OVER:
No one is safe from history
or rash lullabies with facts.

VISUAL:
Mac is in his wan bed when
a green light washes over him,
an emerald baptism, a fire
from green stars finding refuge
in his eyes, a proxy Spring.

VOICE OVER:
A chosen cowboy shadow boxes
an invisible constellation.

VISUAL:
A genius explosion in slow
motion makes the screen
flicker. Roswell glows on
a secret map, a blazing rose.

VOICE OVER:
The only way to smuggle
this poem into the future
is to memorize it. Your
mission has now begun.

VISUAL:
Smoke and sky meet as
Mac looks up—startled
by Prometheus' plunge.
Close-up on Mac bathing in
a tub of long moonlight.
He is a beautiful question.